Easy-to-Make
Stuffed Dinosaurs

by Zillah Halls

DOVER PUBLICATIONS, INC. · New York

Published in Canada by General Publishing Company, Ltd., 30 Lesmill Road, Don Mills, Toronto, Ontario.

Published in the United Kingdom by Constable and Company, Ltd., 10 Orange Street, London WC2H 7EG.

This Dover edition, first published in 1988, is a republication of the work originally published by Dryad Press, Northgates, Leicester (England), in 1972, under the title *Prehistoric Animals*. The text has been reset in a new format and has been edited to eliminate British brand names and terms. The full-size patterns, originally printed on a foldout sheet, have been incorporated into the body of the book.

Manufactured in the United States of America
Dover Publications, Inc., 31 East 2nd Street, Mineola, N.Y. 11501

Library of Congress Cataloging-in-Publication Data

Halls, Zillah.
    Easy-to-make stuffed dinosaurs / by Zillah Halls.
        p.   cm.
    Rev. ed. of: Prehistoric animals. 1st ed. Northgates, Leicester, England : Dryad Press, 1972.
    ISBN 0-486-25848-3 (pbk.)
    1. Soft toy making. 2. Dinosaurs. I. Halls, Zillah. Prehistoric animals. II. Title.
TT174.3.H35   1988
745.592′4—dc19   88-25801
                                                         CIP

Introduction

From the many fossilized remains that have been discovered of the animal (and vegetable) life that populated the earth millions of years ago, paleontologists have pieced together a picture of what life was like on earth before man. Some of the creatures were not unlike some of those we know today—crocodiles, for instance, or fish. Others are so bizarre as to be quite unlike anything we can see now in zoos or in the wild. The story of evolution is a fascinating one, and helps us to understand the complexity and variety of the living creatures which now inhabit the earth.

Many prehistoric animals, now extinct but known to us by their fossilized remains, are easily recreated as soft toys, since they appear to have been fairly simple in shape. The toys are decorative and have some educational value as tangible illustrations of life as it used to be.

The animals have not been designed to a consistent scale; obviously the 40-foot-high Brachiosaurus must be scaled down more than the 3-foot Ichthyostega. Iguanodon has been made on a disproportionately large scale in order to do justice to his three-toed footprint; since numbers of these footprints actually survive, it seemed worthwhile making the animal large enough to show this feature. Ichthyosaurus, however, which grew to about 30 feet long, has been designed as a small toy because it is too simple a shape to look interesting on a large scale in plain fabric. The actual size of all the original animals is stated in the text.

Full-size patterns for the animals are printed in the back of the book. These pattern pieces do *not* include any seam allowance; in most cases, ¼" must be added around each piece before cutting the fabric. A few pattern pieces must be cut without adding seam allowance; this will be noted in the individual instructions. Several of the pattern pieces were too large to fit onto a single page and have been divided into two or three parts. Cut out these pieces and tape them together matching the broken lines and small numbers.

The paper pattern pieces can be pinned directly onto the fabric, or traced to the wrong side of the fabric. Cut the fabric ¼" away from the paper pattern or from the traced line. If you are told to cut two of a pattern piece, be sure to turn the pattern over for the second piece. If you plan to trace around the patterns, you can make them stiffer by gluing them to lightweight cardboard.

A wide variety of fabrics can be used for the toys. A medium-weight woven cotton or cotton-blend fabric is the easiest to work with, but velveteens, velours (such as those used for the models on the covers), corduroys, brocades and satins can all be used effectively. The samples shown inside the book and on the covers were made of solid-color fabrics, or fabrics with a minimal, rather blurred pattern. It was thought that the shapes were sufficiently interesting in themselves and that striking patterns might detract from them. However, there is no reason why a more purely decorative approach should not be taken; Brachiosaurus, for instance, is quite a simply shaped animal and would be attractive made in a flowered print. If you use very thin, slippery or stretchy fabric, baste a lining of lightweight muslin or nonwoven interfacing to the wrong side of each piece.

It is probably easiest to sew the toys together by hand. Although the long, fairly straight seams can be machine-stitched, as was done on the models on the covers, some of the finer shapes would be almost impossible to execute by machine.

There are two ways to approach sewing the toys by hand. For the first method, pin the pieces with the right sides together, and sew ¼" from the edge (or along the traced line) using a running stitch or a back stitch (*Figures 1 and 2*). On curved edges, clip the seam allowance almost to the stitching at intervals; smooth the seam open with your fingers. Continue sewing the toy together, leaving an opening in one seam near the bottom of the toy. Turn the toy right side out.

Figure 1.
Running stitch.

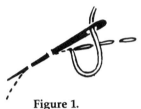

Figure 2.
Backstitch.

In the second method, the one used for most of the models shown and the one described in the individual instructions, the toy is sewn from the right side, eliminating the crumpling that might occur when the piece is turned. For this method, turn the seam allowance of each piece to the wrong side, clipping the curves as necessary; baste in place. Hold the pieces with the wrong sides together and oversew the seam (*Figure 3*), inserting the needle as close to the fold as possible. The stitches will show slightly, but this is perfectly acceptable if the stitches are neat. Be sure to leave an opening near the bottom of the animal to insert the stuffing.

If felt is used for the toys, cut the pieces *without* seam allowances and oversew them together with the cut edges butting. Another possibility is to use plain woven fabric, cutting the pieces without the seam allowance. Paint the cut edges with white glue to prevent their fraying and sew the pieces together as for felt.

In many of the models, features such as teeth and fins are included in the seams. Use a running stitch or a backstitch for these seams, pushing the needle through all three layers. For instance, in the tail fin of Dinichthys, the stitches must pass through the two side pieces and the fin in position between them. Similarly, in the mouth of the same creature, the stitches go through the outer edge of the mouth, the inside of the mouth and, between the two, the teeth.

After the "skin" of the animal is completed, you are ready to stuff the toy. Kapok or old cut-up stockings both work well for stuffing, but polyester fiberfill is probably the most readily available material. Add the stuffing a little bit at a time, molding the animal to the proper shape as you stuff. A wooden skewer, a piece of cane or a blunt crochet hook can be used to push small amounts of stuffing into narrow parts such as feet and tails. A knitting needle is far less satisfactory, as it has a tendency to go right through the stuffing instead of pushing it in place. Bumps and hollows must be corrected as they occur; once the stuffing is completed, they cannot be eliminated except by taking all the stuffing out and starting again. When the animal is firmly stuffed, oversew the opening closed. Take out the basting stitches.

Several animals have separate limbs which are sewn onto the body after both the body and the limbs have been sewn and stuffed. The stitch used for this is either a simple oversewing, or else a blanket stitch (*Figure 4*), which shows more, but is stronger than oversewing.

Eyes are usually shown by stitched-on beads. If

Figure 3.
Oversewing.

Figure 4.
Blanket stitch.

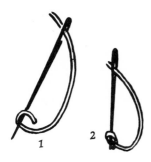

Figure 5.
French knot.

the same thread is used to stitch both eyes, stitching through the head from side to side, eye sockets can be suggested by pulling the thread rather tight. Sometimes a beady eye is suggested by using a bead and nothing else. Other times, the white of the eye is indicated by sewing or gluing on a circle of white felt or fabric; the bead is then sewn on top of this. If the toy is intended for a very young child, you might want to use French knots (*Figure 5*) for eyes rather than beads.

For some animals, such as Dimetrodon or Dinichthys, the teeth are cut from fabric and sewn in; instructions are given with each animal. Other creatures, like Ichthyosaurus and Ichthyostega, have many small teeth; these are best suggested by embroidery as indicated in the individual instructions.

Brachiosaurus

(Shown in color on front cover)

Brachiosaurus was the largest land-dwelling animal that ever lived. A plant-eating reptile, it stood 40 feet high and weighed anywhere from 85 to 100 tons. Brachiosaurus lived in East Africa and North America, and was unusual in having its front legs longer than its hind legs; Diplodocus and Apatosaurus, its contemporaries of comparable size, had back legs larger than their front ones. They all lived in Upper Jurassic times—around 140–150 million years ago.

Cut the pieces as indicated on the patterns. Cut free-form "leaves" from green felt or from woven fabric stiffened with white glue.

Sew the underbody sections to the body sections, matching the small letters and leaving the bottom of each leg open. Sew the soles of the feet in place. Sew the bodies together from A along the top of the head and the back and around the tail to F. Sew the chin gusset in place between A and B, sewing the leaves into the seam, then sew the neck seam from B to E. Sew the underbodies together along the center seam, leaving an opening for stuffing.

Stuff the head very lightly, then take small running stitches through the top of the head as indicated by the broken lines on the pattern (*Figure 1*). Run the ends of the thread to the inside of the animal. Finish stuffing the toy, stuffing the neck very firmly; oversew the opening. If necessary, work a row of running stitches along the back of the neck and pull up the stitches to hold

the neck in the proper position. Fasten off the thread, and run the ends to the inside.

Sew on beads or make French knots for eyes. A warty texture on the back can be suggested by sewing on small beads or by working French knots after the animal is completed.

Figure 1.
To shape the head, take running stitches through the head as indicated on the pattern.

Patterns for Brachiosaurus are on pages 24–25.

Corythosaurus

(Shown in color on back cover)

This dinosaur is a member of the Hadrosauridae family, a family often nicknamed "duck-billed" because of the flattened shape of its jaw. Hadrosaurids were herbivorous and largely land-dwelling, although their webbed feet and flattened tails indicate that they were strong swimmers. One of the most striking features of Corythosaurus is the hollow helmet-shaped extension of its skull and there has been much speculation on its purpose. Corythosaurus grew to about 30 feet tall and probably walked sometimes as a biped, sometimes as a quadruped. It lived in Canada in the Late Cretaceous Period about 70–76 million years ago.

Cut the pieces as indicated on the patterns. If desired, a contrasting fabric may be used for the underbody.

Sew the underbody sections to the body sections, matching the small letters and leaving the bottom of each leg open. Sew the soles of the feet in place. Sew the bodies together from A along the top of the head and the back and around the tail to B. Sew the underbodies together along the center seam, leaving an opening for stuffing.

Stuff the helmet very lightly, then work a row of running stitches across the base of the helmet to keep the stuffing in place. Finish stuffing the toy, molding it carefully to obtain the "duck-bill" shape of the jaw. This area should be kept flat, so do not put too much stuffing into it.

Sew on beads or make French knots for eyes. To keep the front legs from "splaying out" too much, take a few stitches to tack the legs to the underbody at the join.

Patterns for Corythosaurus are on pages 28–29.

Dimetrodon

This reptile lived in what is now Texas in the Permian Period some 240–280 million years ago. It measured up to 11 feet long and was carnivorous, probably attacking and eating its contemporary amphibians. The curious "sail" on its back was a membrane stretched across the spine-like extensions of its vertebrae, and appears to have been a primitive heat-regulating mechanism for the cold-blooded reptile. If the animal stood with its sail facing the sun, it would absorb heat from its rays; if, on the other hand, it stood with its sail in line with the sun's rays, it would absorb very little heat.

Cut the body, underbody and sail as indicated on the pattern pieces (do not add seam allowances to the sail); a contrasting fabric may be used for the underbody if desired. Cut the inside mouth from red fabric or felt, the teeth from white felt or fabric stiffened with glue (do not add seam allowances to the teeth).

Glue fine cord or very thick thread to the wrong side of one sail piece along the lines indicated for the ribs (*Figure 1*). With the wrong sides together, glue the other sail to this piece (*Figure 2*). When the glue is thoroughly dry, trim the sail as shown on the pattern (*Figure 3*).

Tack the bodies together at A. Baste the teeth to the body and underbody. Fold the mouth along the broken line and baste it to the jaws. Sew the jaw seam with small running stitches passing through all the layers (*Figures 4 and 5*). Stitch the bodies together along the top edge from A to E, inserting the sail into the seam between C and D.

To attach the sail, take small running stitches through all three pieces—the two bodies and the sail. Sew the underbody to the body, leaving an opening for stuffing on one side.

Particularly careful stuffing is needed for the open mouth and for the positioning of the limbs. The animal has a straddling posture, rather like a crocodile. This effect is achieved by stuffing the legs firmly between the joints, but lightly enough at the joints themselves to leave some flexibility in the legs.

Sew on beads or make French knots for eyes.

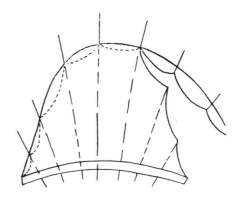

Figure 3.
Trim the top edge of the sail.

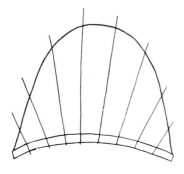

Figure 1.
Glue cord or thick thread to one layer to indicate ribs.

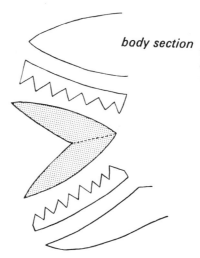

Figure 4.
Baste the teeth, then the inside mouth to the body and underbody sections.

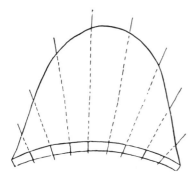

Figure 2.
Glue the second layer to the first—the ribs are now covered but still appear in outline.

Figure 5.
The finished mouth.

Patterns for Dimetrodon are on pages 32–33.

Dinichthys

This was a primitive fish living in the Devonian Period, 345–395 million years ago. Fish even more primitive than this one were clothed in bony armor; having discarded this, Dinichthys was more mobile than they and had jaws strong enough to crack open the armor of its contemporaries, on whom it preyed. It grew to about 30 feet long.

Cut the body and base as indicated on the pattern pieces; cut the mouth from red felt or fabric. Do not add seam allowances to the teeth or the fins. Cut the teeth from white felt or fabric stiffened with glue. To cut the fins, glue two layers of fabric together with the wrong sides in. When the glue is dry, cut the fins as indicated on the patterns.

Starting at C, sew the bodies together along the top edge for about 1"; tack the bodies together at A. Baste the teeth to the upper and lower mouth, then baste the inside mouth in place. Join with small running stitches through all layers (*Figures 1 and 2*). Sew the base to the body sections, matching the small letters and inserting a front fin into the seam on each side; leave an opening for stuffing on one side. Continue sewing the bodies together, inserting the back fins between J and K (hold the fins together and insert as one piece), the bottom tail fin between F and G and the top tail fin between D and E (*Figures 3 and 4*). Stuff firmly and close the opening.

Cut two small eye circles of white felt, iron-on interfacing or fabric stiffened with glue. Sew, fuse or glue the circles to the head; sew a bead or make a French knot in the center of each circle.

Patterns for Dinichthys are on page 64.

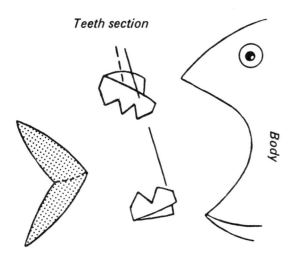

Figure 1.
Baste the teeth, then the inside mouth to the upper and lower mouth.

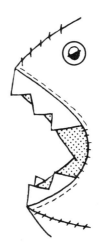

Figure 2.
The finished mouth.

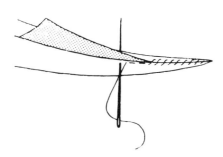

Figure 3.
Insert the fins into the seam and attach with running stitches passing through both body and fin.

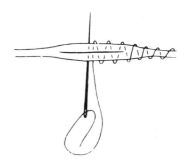

Figure 4.
Top view of attaching tail fin.

Diplocaulus

(Shown in color on back cover)

Diplocaulus was an amphibian, 2 to 3 feet long, which lived in Texas 260 to 280 million years ago in Early Permian times. It probably lived at the bottom of lakes and ponds. The reason for the curious broad-arrow shape of its head is unknown.

Cut the pieces as indicated on the patterns. The two body sections may be cut from contrasting fabrics if desired. Cut the inside mouth from red fabric or felt. Sew the body sections together along the top of the head, leaving an opening between A and B. Do not sew the remainder of the body together at this time. Sew the inside mouth to the body, matching the small letters. Finish sewing the body sections together, leaving an opening for stuffing.

Stuff the animal, stuffing the mouth area carefully to produce the open shape. For teeth, embroider tiny straight stitches along the edge of the mouth, using 3 to 4 strands of white embroidery floss. Cut eye circles from white felt, iron-on interfacing or fabric stiffened with glue; attach to the animal. Sew a bead or make a French knot in the center of each eye circle.

Patterns for Diplocaulus are on pages 36–37.

Geosaurus

This was a crocodile that went back to live in the sea. Land-dwelling crocodiles of various kinds, with properly developed limbs, had already evolved; but the limbs of Geosaurus have become seal-like flippers or paddles and its tail has become a fish tail. It lived in Upper Jurassic times, about 146 million years ago, and grew up to about 15 feet long.

Cut the pieces as indicated on the patterns. The underbody and the undersides of the paddles may be cut from contrasting fabric if desired.

First, sew the side sections to the top of the body, matching the letters carefully; then sew the underbody to the top and sides, leaving an opening for stuffing. Sew the tail sections together from B to C. Stuff the body firmly. Sew the paddles together in pairs, leaving them open between the letters at the short curved edge. Stuff the paddles, then sew them to the body, matching the letters. The upper curve of the paddle should be sewn above the seam, the lower curve below it (*Figure 1*).

Sew on large sequins for eye circles; sew a bead or make a French knot in the center of each.

Figure 1.
Sew the top curve of the paddle above the seam, the lower curve below the seam.

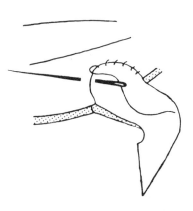

Patterns for Geosaurus are on pages 40–41.

Ichthyosaurus

This was a fishlike animal which was, in fact, a reptile adapted for life in the sea, just as the whales of today are not fishes, but mammals similarly adapted. The reptiles' limbs, which originally evolved from fishes' fins, have now become paddles. Ichthyosaurus was very successful, growing up to 30 feet long. It was common in the Lower Jurassic Period, about 185 million years ago.

Cut the pieces as indicated on the patterns. The base can be a contrasting fabric if desired.

Sew the fins together. Sew the bodies together from A along the top edge and around the tail to B, inserting the fin between C and D. Sew the base to the body, leaving an opening for stuffing. Stuff the tail lightly, then stitch along the lines indicated on the pattern to keep the stuffing in place. Finish stuffing the animal. Careful stuffing is needed to insure that the paddles stick out horizontally. Alternatively, they can be made separately and sewn into the side seam the way the fin is included in the top seam.

Cut eye circles from white felt, interfacing or fabric stiffened with glue; attach to the head. With three strands of dark gray embroidery floss, work straight stitches from the center to the edge of each circle as indicated on the pattern.

Work white straight stitches along the long narrow jaw for the teeth. Embroider the mouth in dark gray chain stitch (*Figure 1*).

Figure 1.
Chain stitch.

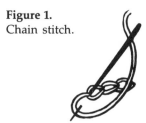

Patterns for Ichthyosaurus are on page 44.

Ichthyostega

(Shown in color on back cover)

Ichthyostega, one of the first amphibians, lived in Greenland during the Late Devonian Period, about 350 million years ago. The amphibians evolved from the lobe-finned fish. These had primitive lungs and a fairly complex bone structure in their fins. Once these fish had ventured onto land, as their lungs enabled them to do, the fins gradually developed into limbs and the lungs became more efficient. So the amphibians, the first land-dwelling creatures (who, nevertheless, spent much of their time in the water), had arrived. Ichthyostega grew to about 3 feet long.

Cut all of the pieces except the tail fin as indicated on the patterns. A contrasting fabric may be used for the underbody and the underside of the legs. Do not add seam allowances to the tail fin. Glue two layers of fabric with the wrong sides together; when the glue is dry, cut the tail fin.

Sew the top of the body to the side sections, matching the small letters. Sew the side sections together from C to the tip, inserting the tail fin in the seam. Sew the underbody to the top and sides, leaving an opening for stuffing. Stuff the animal firmly. Sew the legs together in pairs, leaving open between the small letters. Stuff the legs, stuffing the feet very lightly so that they will stay flat and rest on the ground. Pin the legs to the body, matching the letters. Sew in place, sewing the top surface above the side seam and the lower surface below the seam (*Figure 1*).

Sew on beads or make French knots for eyes. Embroider a brown chain-stitch (*Figure 2*) mouth along the seam at the head; add white straight-stitch teeth.

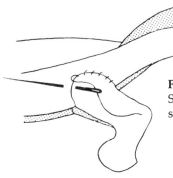

Figure 1.
Sew the top curve of the legs above the side seam, the lower curve below the seam.

Figure 2.
Chain stitch.

Patterns for Ichthyostega are on page 45.

Iguanodon

(Shown in color on front cover)

This herbivorous dinosaur lived in Early Cretaceous times, 115–135 million years ago. It is known to have lived in western Europe, Romania, western North America, North Africa and Mongolia. It grew to about 16 feet in height. The characteristic spiky thumbs were probably weapons of defense.

Cut the pieces as indicated on the patterns, cutting the body front and the inside of the arms from a contrasting fabric if desired. To cut the dewlap, place the arrow on the straight grain of the fabric.

Starting at C and ending at J, sew the body front sections to the body sections. Sew the back of the legs together from M to H to M; leave the bottom of each foot open. Sew on the soles of the feet. Sew the body sections to the top of the head. Sew the back seam from A around the tail to H. Fold the dewlap along the broken line with the right sides out (*Figure 1*). Sew the center front seam from B to H, inserting the dewlap between D and E and leaving an opening for stuffing.

Stuff the animal. Be careful to stuff the thigh firmly. If necessary, take a few stitches through the body at the thigh to shape it. Work a row of running stitches along the top edge of the tail between F and G; pull up the stitches so that the animal stands properly.

Sew the arms together in pairs, leaving an opening for stuffing. Stuff firmly. Sew the arms to the body as indicated on the pattern, positioning them as desired (*Figure 2*).

Embroider a chain-stitch mouth and silver satin-stitch "hooves" (*Figure 3*). For each eye, cut a large sequin into a long narrow shape (fabric could also be used) and sew it to the head; sew a bead or make a French knot in the center of this.

Patterns for Iguanodon are on pages 48–49.

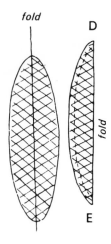

Figure 1.
Fold dewlap in half with right side out and insert raw edges into the center seam.

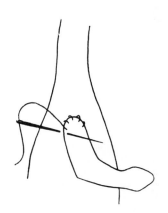

Figure 2.
Sew the arms to the body.

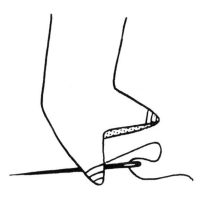

Figure 3.
Embroider satin-stitch hooves on the top of each foot.

Kuehneosaurus

(Shown in color on back cover)

Kuehneosaurus was a lizard, about 1½ to 2½ feet long, that lived in Great Britain. Remains of a very similar animal, called Icarosaurus, have also been found in the eastern United States. Kuehneosaurus and Icarosaurus lived in Late Triassic or Early Jurassic times, about 180–200 million years ago. The "wings" were extensions of the ribs with an attached membrane, rather like the "sail" of the Dimetrodon. It could have glided several feet from the height of a tree.

Do not add seam allowances to the wing pattern. Cut the pieces as indicated on the patterns; the underbody may be cut from a contrasting fabric if desired.

Glue fine cord or very thick thread to the wrong side of two wings along the lines indicated for ribs. With wrong sides together, glue the plain wings to the "ribbed" wings. When dry, trim to shape (*see Dimetrodon, Figures 1, 2 and 3, page 9*).

On the body and underbody, clip the seam allowance to the stitching line at the broken lines on the feet; do not turn in the seam allowance on the feet. Sew the body and underbody together to the base of the tail, inserting the wings into the seam. Leave the tail unstitched and leave the feet free below the broken lines. Stitch along the broken lines at the base of the feet through all layers. Stuff the upper portion of the body firmly. Sew one side of the tail from the base to the tip. Sew the other side, stuffing as you go. Glue the two layers of the feet together; when the glue is dry, trim to shape.

Sew on beads or make French knots for eyes.

Patterns for Kuehneosaurus are on page 52.

Plateosaurus

This was one of the first of the dinosaurs. Plateosaurus lived on a plant diet in Western Europe about 200 million years ago in Triassic times. It was about 20 to 25 feet long. Plateosaurus probably walked on all fours, but could rear up on its hind legs to browse.

Cut the pieces as indicated on the patterns. Sew the underbody sections to the body sections from E to D and from C to F; leave the bottom of the feet open. Sew the soles of the feet in place. Sew the gusset to the body sections matching the small letters. Sew the body sections together from B to E and from A along the back and around the tail to F. Sew the underbodies together along the center, leaving an opening for stuffing.

Stuff the animal firmly. The gusset under the chin will give the head its flattened shape. Very careful modeling is needed for the hind legs. Stuff very firmly, then sew through the body from side to side to indicate the contour of the thigh (*Figure 1*).

Sew the arms together in pairs, stuff, then sew to the body (*Figure 2*).

Sew on beads or make French knots for eyes.

Patterns for Plateosaurus are on page 53.

Figure 1.
Stitch through the leg to
  shape the thigh.

Figure 2.
Sew the arms to the body.

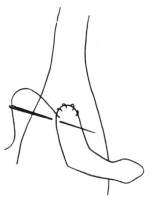

Shansisuchus

(Shown in color on back cover)

This was an early archosaur—a member of the reptile family that would eventually evolve, not only into the dinosaurs and pterodactyls of the past, but also into today's snakes, lizards, crocodiles and birds. Shansisuchus lived in China in Lower Triassic times, about 225 million years ago, and was about 10 feet long. Its powerful jaws and teeth suggest it was carnivorous.

Cut the pieces as indicated on the patterns, placing the broken line of the underbody on the fold of the fabric. The underbody may be cut from contrasting fabric if desired. Cut the inside mouth from red fabric or felt. Do not add seam allowances to the teeth; cut from white felt, interfacing or fabric stiffened with glue.

Cut the body pieces along the mouth line and paint the fabric edges with glue. Allow to dry. Sew the bodies to the head gusset, matching the letters; sew the bodies together from B to D. Baste the teeth, then the inside mouth into the mouth opening; sew through all layers with small running stitches (*see Dimetrodon, Figures 4 and 5, page 9*). Oversew the corners of the mouth. Sew the underbody to the bodies, leaving the bottom of the feet open. Sew the bodies together from C along the back and around the tail to E. Stuff the body firmly through the leg openings. Sew the soles of the feet in place.

Sew on beads or make French knots for eyes. A warty texture of the skin can be suggested by sewing beads or making French knots on the animal's back after it is stuffed.

Patterns for Shansisuchus are on pages 56–57.

Triceratops

(Shown in color on front cover)

This was among the last of the dinosaurs and was very common in North America in Upper Cretaceous times, about 65–75 million years ago. They were large herbivores, 20 to 30 feet long, and were protected by their three rhinoceros-like horns and the frill of bone projecting up over the neck from the skull.

Cut the pieces as indicated on the patterns. The underbody, the soles of the feet and the horns may be cut from contrasting fabrics if desired. Pin the underbody sections to the body sections, matching the small E's and B's. Sew, leaving the bottom of the feet open. Sew the soles of the feet in place. Sew the body sections together from B around the head, along the back and around the tail to E. Sew the center seam of the underbody, leaving an opening for stuffing. Stuff firmly and close the opening.

Sew the neck frill sections together along the center, leaving an opening for the nose horn. Cut

Figure 1.
To shape the head, take running stitches through the head as indicated on the pattern.

holes for the side horns as indicated on the patterns. Sew the facing to the neck frill by blanket-stitching from C to D and along the scalloped outside edge. Assemble the horns by sewing the long straight edges together. Stuff firmly; insert into the holes in the neck frill and sew securely.

Slip the neck frill over the head and sew it to the head from A to C. Sew the facing to the neck (*Figure 1*).

Sew on beads or make French knots for eyes. Sew beads or make French knots over the back to suggest the warty texture of the skin.

Patterns for Triceratops are on pages 60–61.

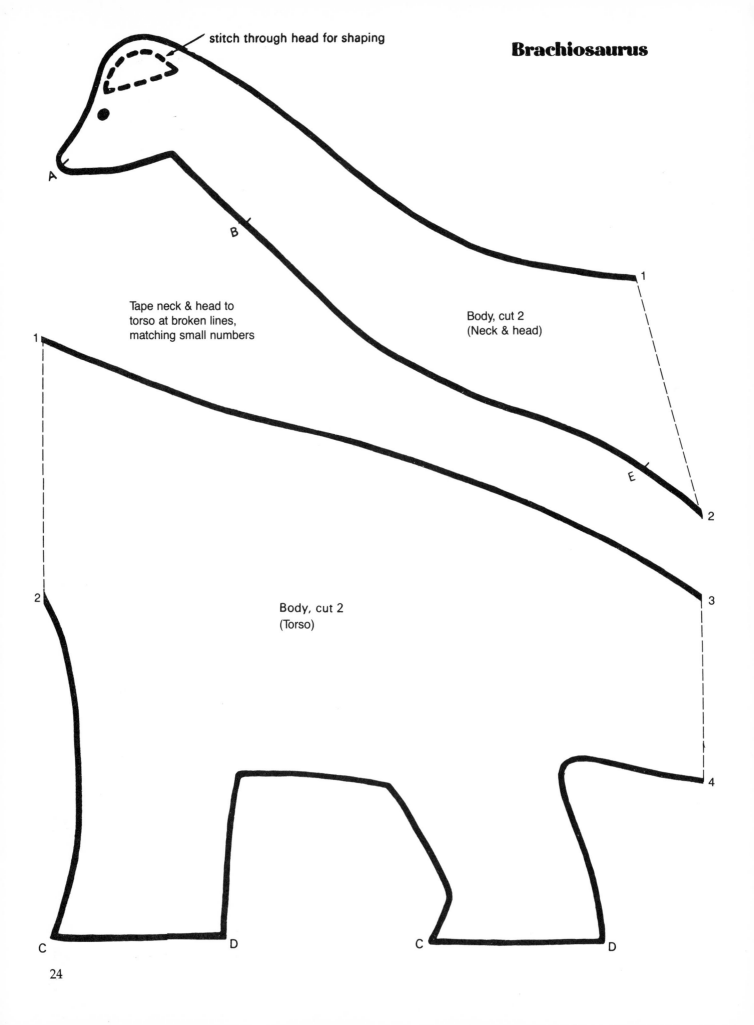

stitch through head for shaping

Brachiosaurus

A

B

Body, cut 2
(Neck & head)

1

Tape neck & head to
torso at broken lines,
matching small numbers

E

2

1

Body, cut 2
(Torso)

3

2

4

C

D

C

D

24

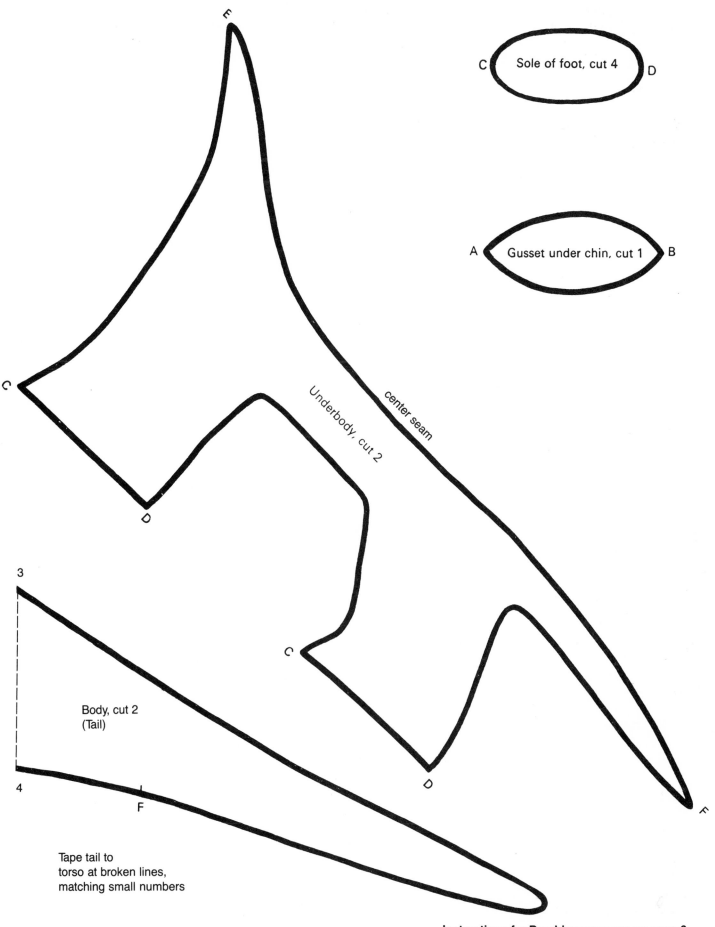

E

C Sole of foot, cut 4 D

A Gusset under chin, cut 1 B

center seam

Underbody, cut 2

C

C

D

3

Body, cut 2
(Tail)

4

F

D

F

Tape tail to
torso at broken lines,
matching small numbers

Instructions for Brachiosaurus are on page 6.

Corythosaurus

Body, cut 2

stitch line

A

B

28

Sole of front feet, cut 2

Sole of back feet, cut 2

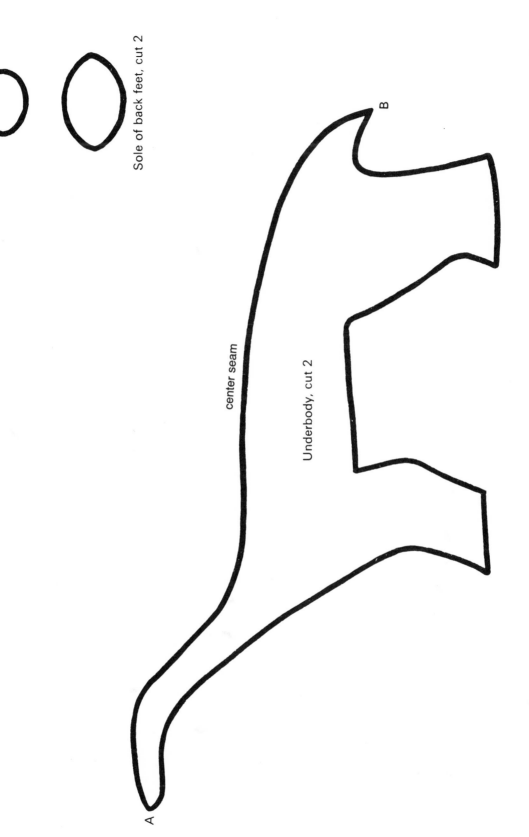

center seam

Underbody, cut 2

A

B

Instructions for Corythosaurus are on page 7.

Dimetrodon

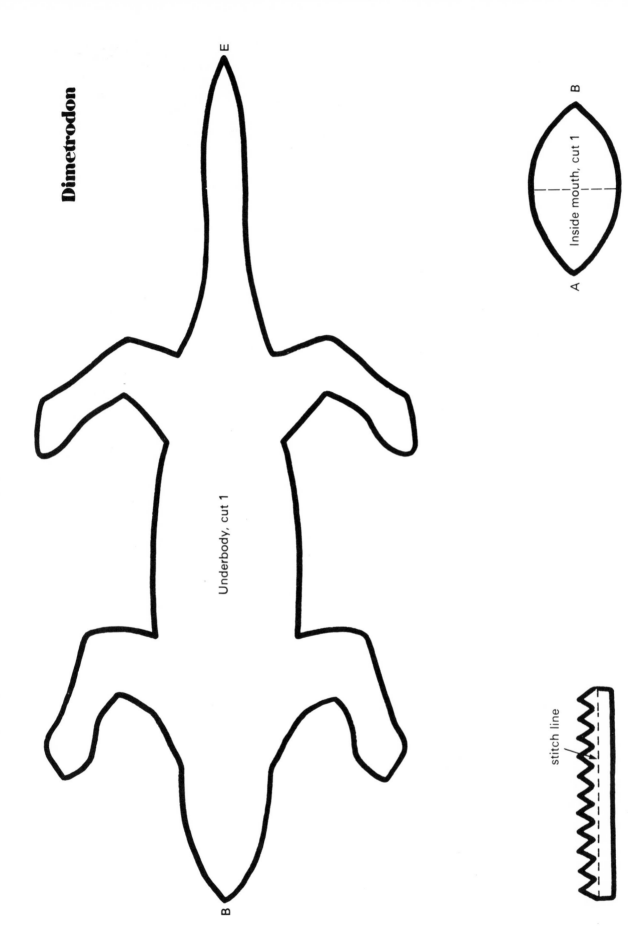

Underbody, cut 1

Inside mouth, cut 1

stitch line

Teeth, cut 2

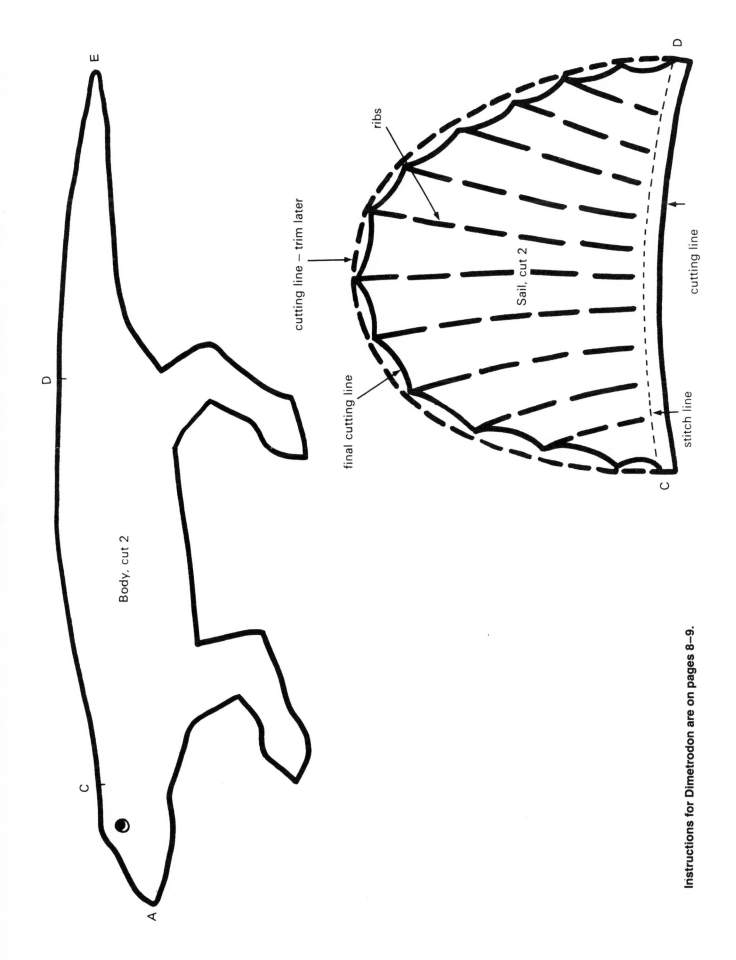

Body, cut 2

ribs

Sail, cut 2

cutting line – trim later

final cutting line

cutting line

stitch line

Instructions for Dimetrodon are on pages 8–9.

Diplocaulus

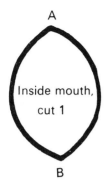

A

Inside mouth,
cut 1

B

1

2

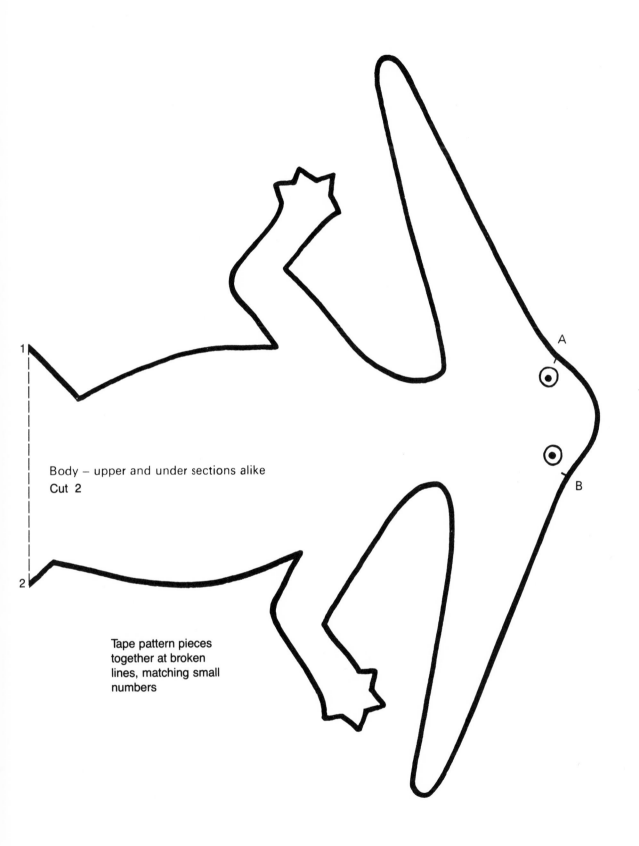

1

Body – upper and under sections alike
Cut 2

A

B

Tape pattern pieces
together at broken
lines, matching small
numbers

2

Instructions for Diplocaulus are on page 12.

Geosaurus

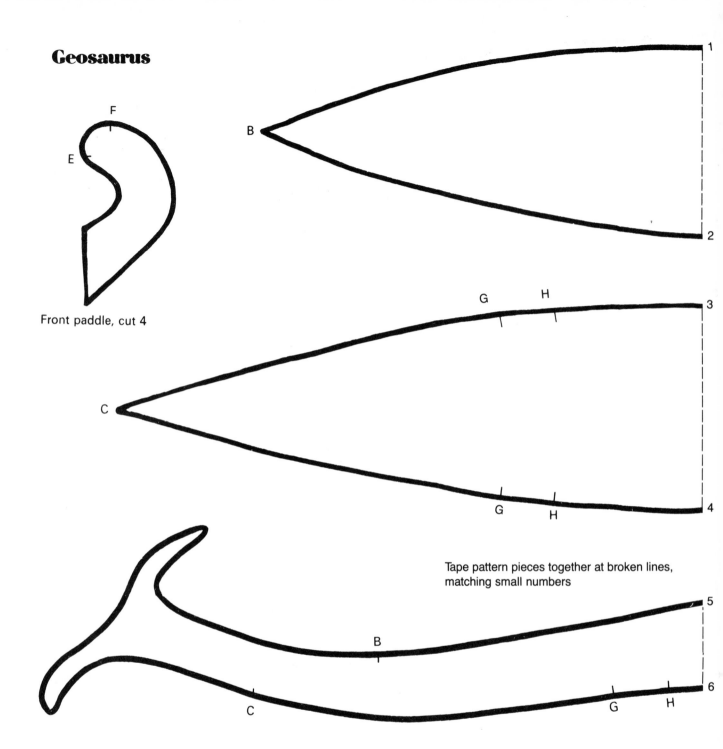

Front paddle, cut 4

Tape pattern pieces together at broken lines, matching small numbers

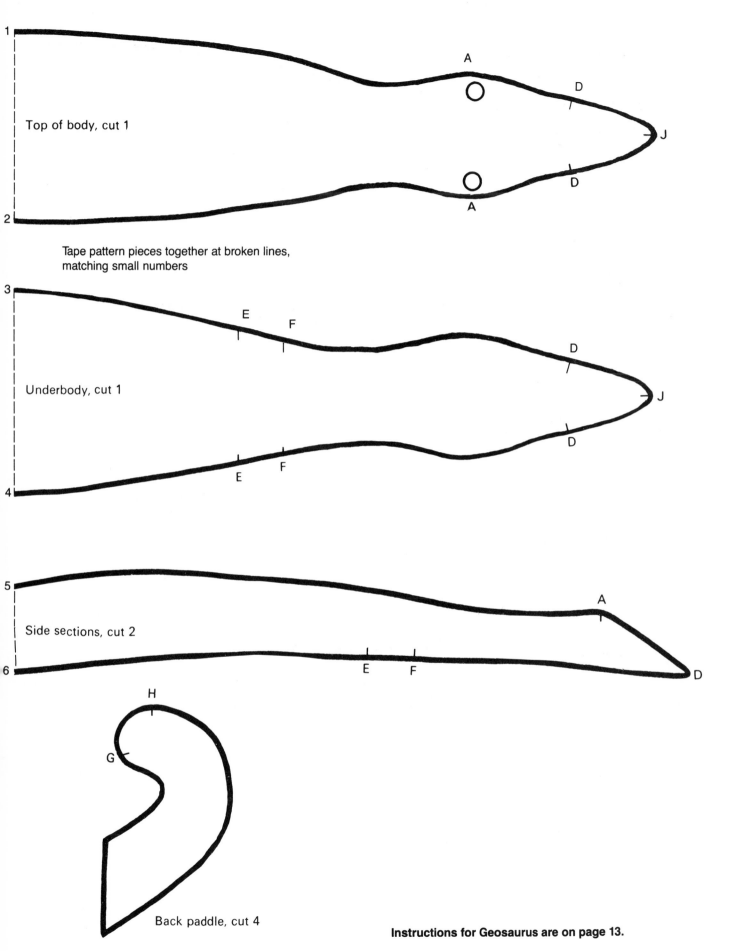

Top of body, cut 1

A
D
J
D
A

Tape pattern pieces together at broken lines,
matching small numbers

Underbody, cut 1

E
F
D
J
D
E
F

Side sections, cut 2

A
E
F
D

H
G

Back paddle, cut 4

Instructions for Geosaurus are on page 13.

Ichthyosaurus

Base, cut 1

Body, cut 2

Fin, cut 2

stitch line

stitch line

Instructions for Ichthyosaurus are on page 14.

44

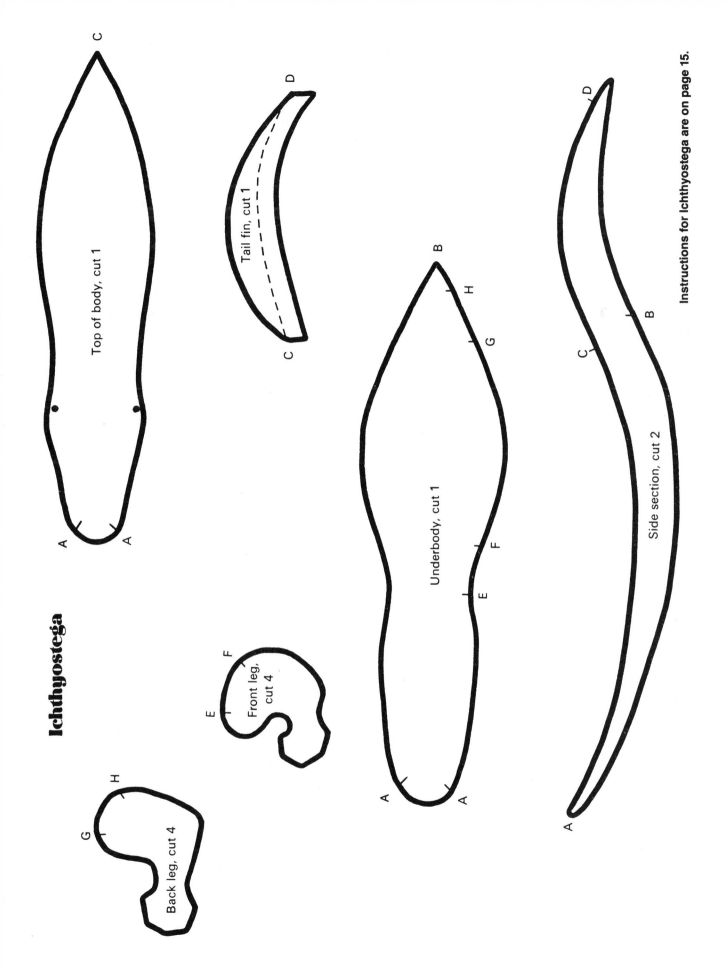

Ichthyostega

Top of body, cut 1

Tail fin, cut 1

Underbody, cut 1

Front leg, cut 4

Back leg, cut 4

Side section, cut 2

Instructions for Ichthyostega are on page 15.

45

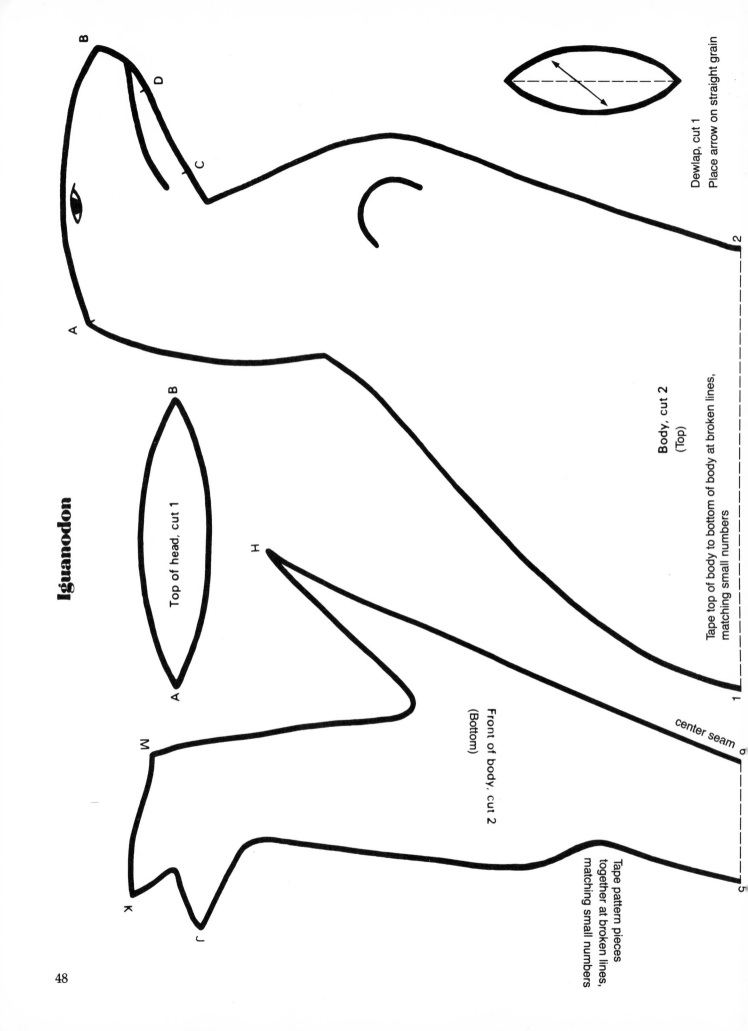

Iguanodon

Top of head, cut 1

Dewlap, cut 1
Place arrow on straight grain

Body, cut 2
(Top)

Tape top of body to bottom of body at broken lines, matching small numbers

Front of body, cut 2
(Bottom)

center seam

Tape pattern pieces together at broken lines, matching small numbers

48

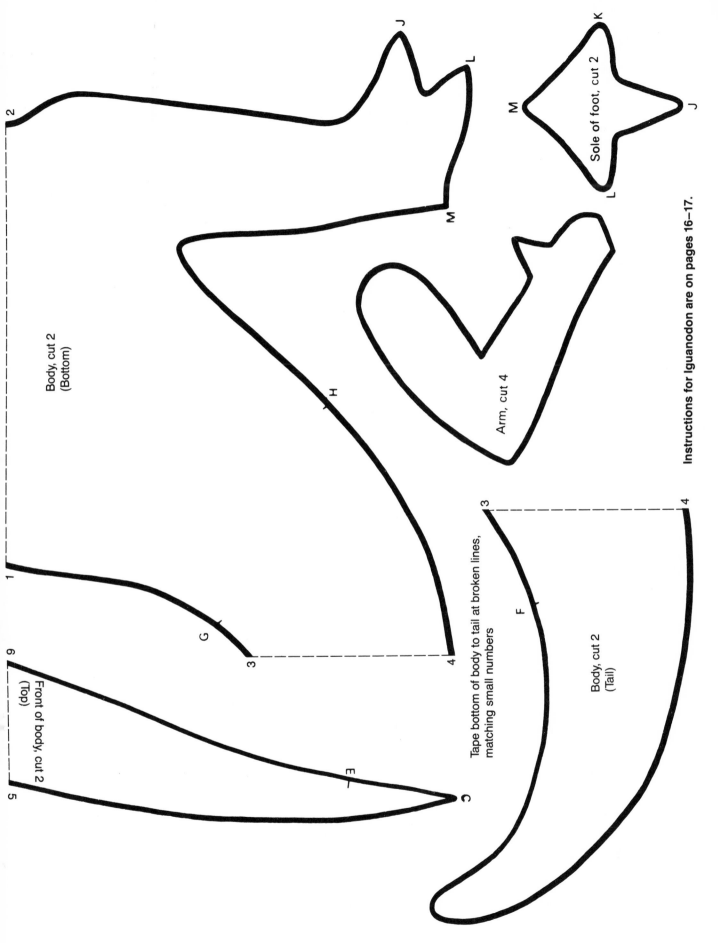

Body, cut 2
(Bottom)

Sole of foot, cut 2

Arm, cut 4

Instructions for Iguanodon are on pages 16–17.

Tape bottom of body to tail at broken lines, matching small numbers

Body, cut 2
(Tail)

Front of body, cut 2
(Top)

Kuehneosaurus

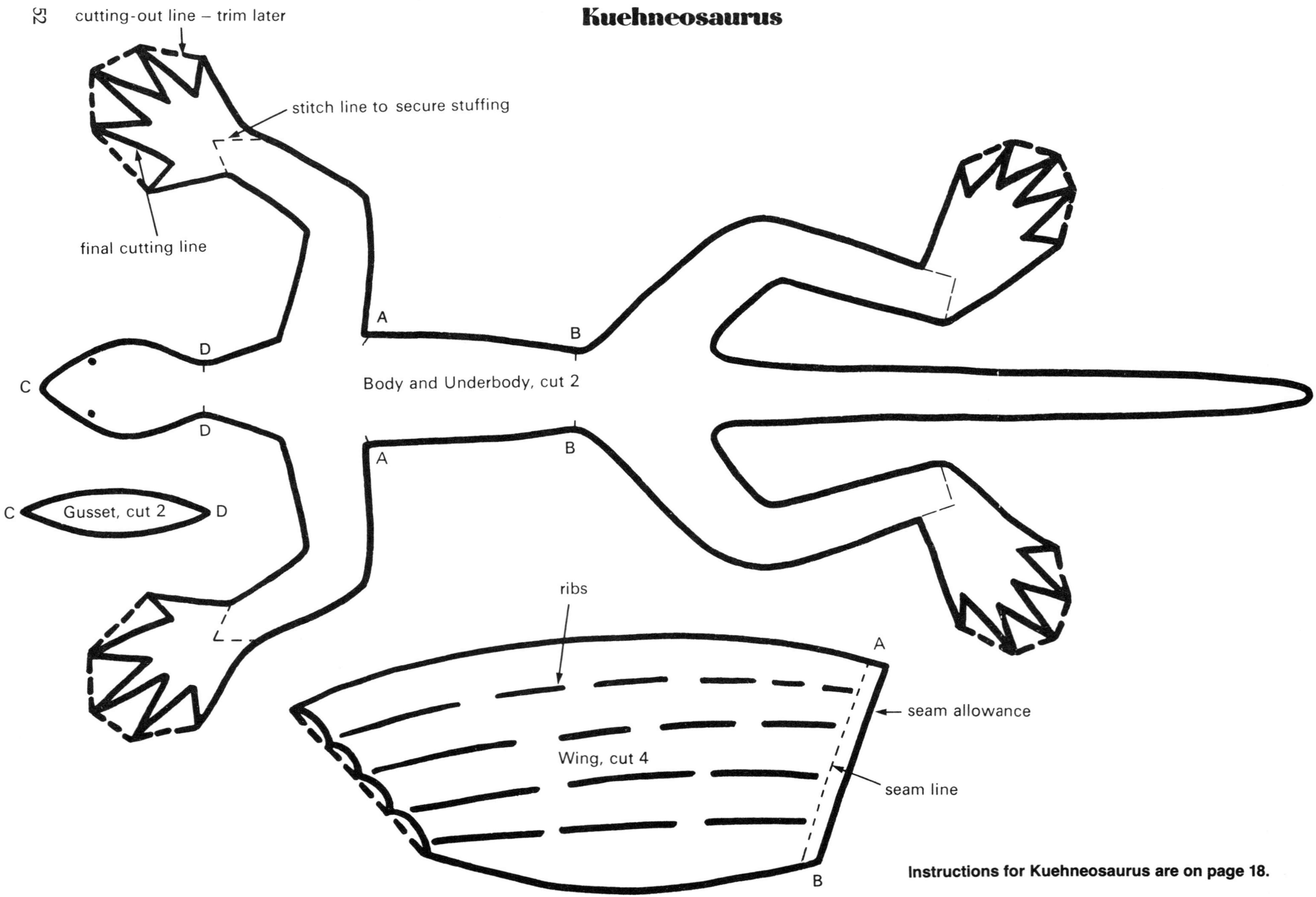

cutting-out line – trim later

stitch line to secure stuffing

final cutting line

A

B

Body and Underbody, cut 2

B

A

D D D

C C

Gusset, cut 2

ribs

Wing, cut 4

seam allowance

seam line

A

B

Instructions for Kuehneosaurus are on page 18.

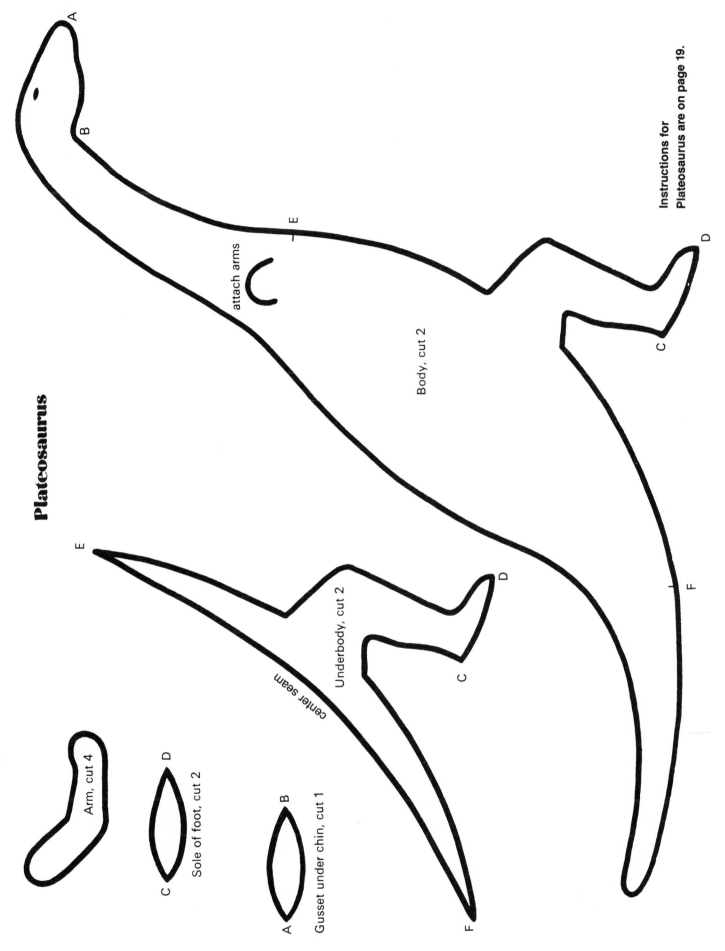

Plateosaurus

attach arms

Body, cut 2

Underbody, cut 2

center seam

Arm, cut 4

Sole of foot, cut 2

Gusset under chin, cut 1

Instructions for Plateosaurus are on page 19.

Shansisuchus

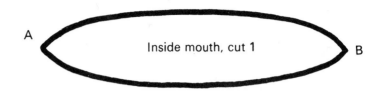

A   Inside mouth, cut **1**   B

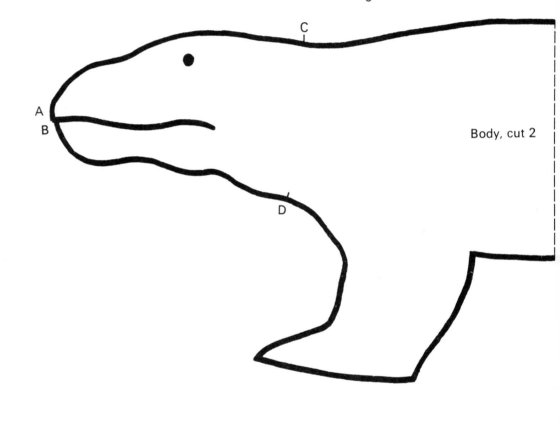

Tape pattern pieces together at broken lines, matching small numbers

C

A
B

D

Body, cut 2

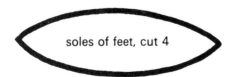

soles of feet, cut 4

Instructions for Shansisuchus are on page 20.

Teeth, cut 2

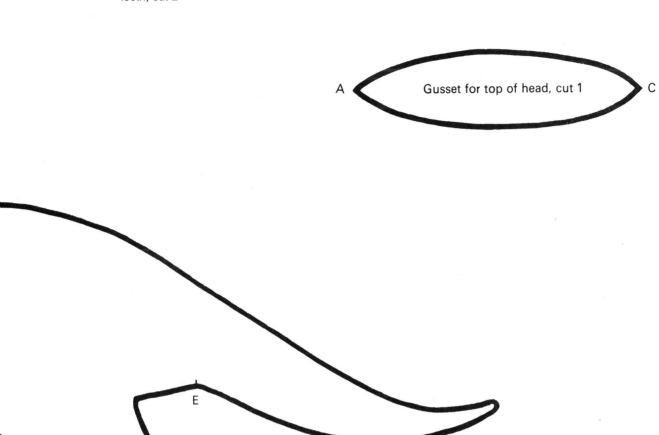

A   Gusset for top of head, cut 1   C

E

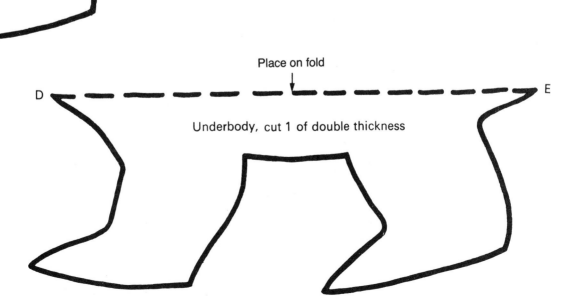

Place on fold

D   E

Underbody, cut 1 of double thickness

Nose horn, cut 1

Side horn, cut 2

Triceratops

center seam

Side horn, cut 2

Neck frill. cut 2

nose horn

A B C D

Neck frill facing, cut 1

C D D C

Body, cut 2

1

2

E

Tape pattern pieces together
at broken lines,
matching small numbers

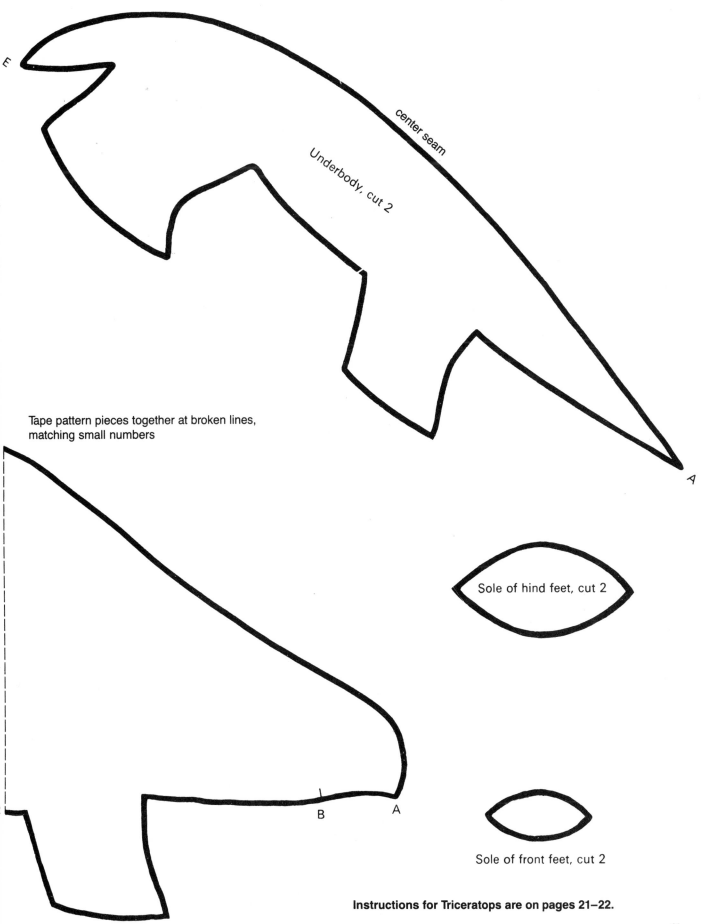

center seam

Underbody, cut 2

E

A

Tape pattern pieces together at broken lines,
matching small numbers

Sole of hind feet, cut 2

B   A

Sole of front feet, cut 2

Instructions for Triceratops are on pages 21–22.

Dinichthys

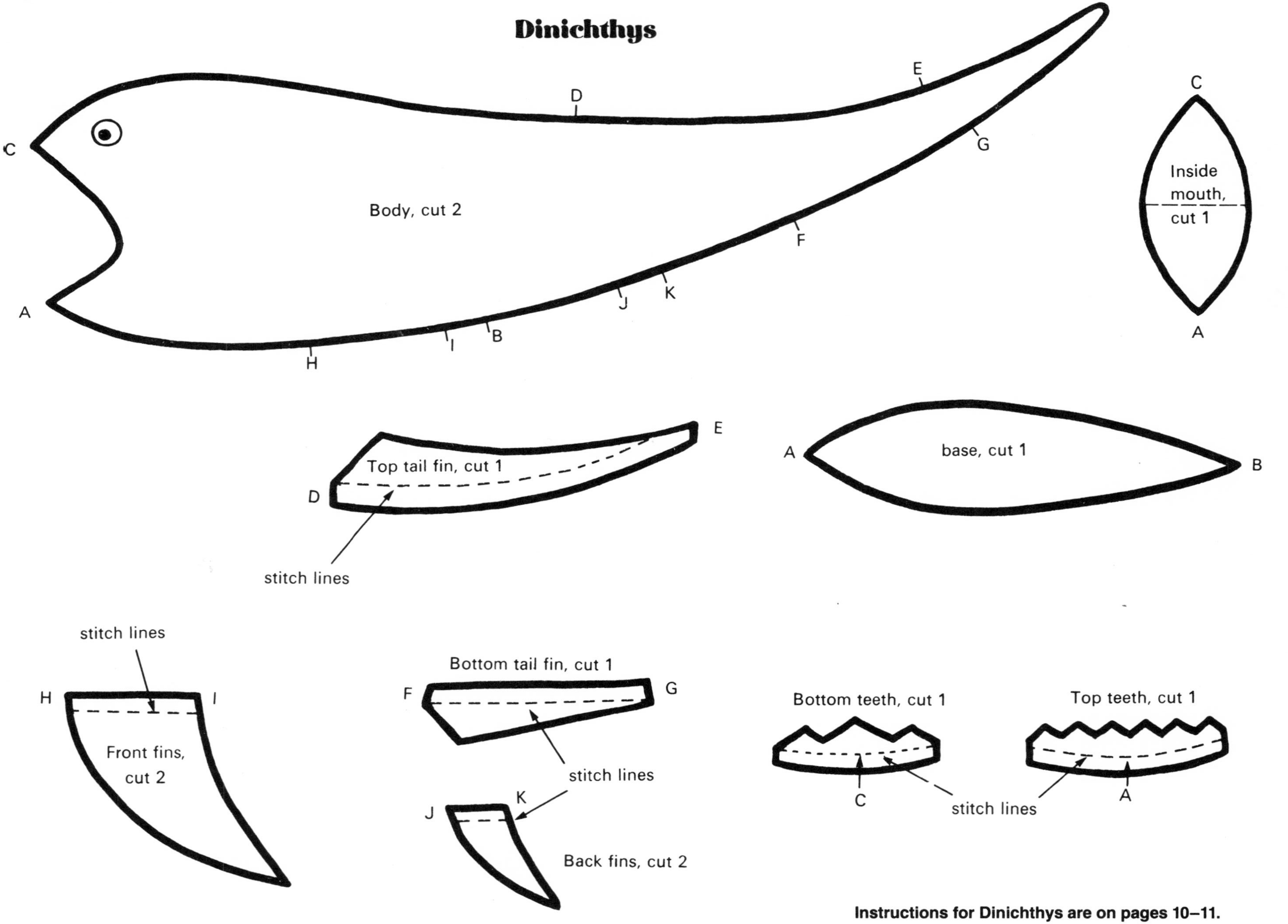

Body, cut 2

C

A

G

E

D

F

K

J

B

I

H

C

Inside mouth, cut 1

A

B

base, cut 1

A

Top teeth, cut 1

A

stitch lines

Bottom teeth, cut 1

C

Instructions for Dinichthys are on pages 10–11.

E

Top tail fin, cut 1

stitch lines

D

G

Bottom tail fin, cut 1

stitch lines

F

Back fins, cut 2

K

J

I

stitch lines

Front fins, cut 2

H